Swimming the Witch

Swimming the Witch

Poems by Leilani Hall

Cherry Grove Collections

Published by Cherry Grove Collections
P.O. Box 541106
Cincinnati, OH 45254-1106

Typeset in Classical Garamond by WordTech Communications LLC,
Cincinnati, OH

ISBN: 1932339906
LCCN: 2004116060

Poetry Editor: Kevin Walzer
Business Editor: Lori Jareo

Visit us on the web at www.cherry-grove.com

Acknowledgments

Grateful acknowledgement is made to the following journals in which some of the poems in this manuscript have previously appeared: *The Mississippi Review, Hamlet Anniversary Edition*: "Ophelia's Rant Before She's Heavy With Drink"; *The Laurel Review*: "Tattooed," "To a Pulaski County Prisoner," and "Women in Rooms, Room I," which appeared as "December Havanaise, Lento"; *The Ohio Review*: "Venerari"; *The Journal*: "Half-Hanged Mary Dreams Only Last Lines of Poetry," which appeared in variant form as "Clara Shepherd Lives in Spencer, West Virginia, Where She Writes Only the Last Lines of Poetry"; *Poet Lore*: "Letter to the Postmaster"; *The Hawaii Review*: "Mourner at the River" and "Appendix," which appeared as "The Other Lesson"; *New Orleans Review*: "Sacra Via"; *The Cortland Review*: "Final Notes," which appeared as "Random Communication," "Utility," and "Before Learning the Imperial War Museum Was Once Bedlam"; *Riverwind*: "Limb by Limb," which appeared as "The Last Child, 1953"; *Spillway*: "The Nudge Photograph," which appeared in variant form as "Figure," and "Exercise of Grief"; *ICON*: "Serpent Handling," which appeared in variant form; *The Chattahoochee Review*: "Lost Sight"; *Water~Stone*: "For Josh Who Thought He Would Not Turn Seven"; *Word Journal*: "How it Passes," "Woman Trapping," and "The Last Labor, Trial by Water"; *Poetry East*: "Unspoken"

I am grateful to California State University-Northridge for the time and support to complete this manuscript. I would also like to thank Angela Ball, D.C. Berry, Frederick Barthelme, Wayne Dodd, Dorothy Barresi, Dr. Susan Young, Dr. Virginia Crawford, and Tina Hall, without whose help this book would not have been possible. This book exists in loving memory of Tom Andrews and A.T. Hall Jr., who walked beyond the boundaries of illness.

for Bailey
who rescued me from the water

III

Letter from Sussex

Many hundred thousand good-nights, dear reader. Innocent have I come into prison, innocent must I die. For whoever comes into the witch prison must become a witch or be tortured until she invents something out of her head and—God pity her—bethinks her of something. When I was first time put to the torture, a priest and doctor came to me with small pouches of salt about their necks, crossing themselves in holy and averting their eyes from mine. The priest asked, "Woman, how come you here?" I answered, "Through falsehood, through misfortune. I am no witch." Now Peter of Tothweil was set before me who certified that I floated on a single branch in water, willing it to turn on my song, and afterward the neighbor's children came forward, who had spied me running downhill calling my milk bucket hither to follow. Then six men from the congregation stepped forward to say that I had caused the miller's son to fall from the steps by glance of eye, and that after his fall, when I ran to help, my touch on his back sent him to bed stricken with loss of breath until his death. And then came also—God in highest Heaven have mercy—the executioner, and put me in the icy well to see that I should float or drown. When I did but keep my head above the water, they stripped me and bound both my hands together, so that the blood ran out at the wrists, and thereafter shaved my head with the blade such that I suffered terribly. When at last the executioner led me back into the prison, he said to me: "For God's sake confess something, where it be true or not. Invent something, for you cannot endure the torture you will be put to; say you are a witch." And so I confessed, invented that I was to kill my children, but killed a horse instead. It did not help to gain my release. At final, I confessed I had taken a sacred wafer and desecrated it in the horse's urine so that my husband's sister Sarah may not come to bear a child. Now you have all my confession, invention for which I must die, so help me God. Dear reader, keep this letter secret so that people do not find it, else you shall be tortured most piteously and the jailers will be beheaded. So strictly is it forbidden. Please, dear reader, pay this man a token who has delivered this note to you. I am in a sad plight to burn today. Will never see you more.

22 July 1628

I

Is this voice—remnant hum of the living,
message replayed—sufficient? Will this syntax
keep (forbidden or preserved) promise from fact?

How It Passes

for Tina, who chose not to

I speak of salt, that I have rubbed it
into my child's lips for good health,
put her to bed after dinner, told her to think
of Elisha who cast salt into a spring to save it.
I have tried to save everything—
the button on my husband's cuff,
the cornish game hens in the oven,
my son's blundered homework.
But my days open like eggs cracked
before I touch them, and the bougainvillea
that spills its red over the kitchen window
is another skinned knee I cannot heal.

No wonder my fevered daughter stood last evening
in the doorway behind me, her nightgown
hanging white to the ankles. No wonder
she begged me not to turn around, having dreamed
of Lot's wife, her lips dry and furrowed, parched.

Station of Loss

Thus ended this woman her miserable life,
after she had lived many years poor, wretched,
scorned and forsaken of the world.
> —Record of Execution for Helen Jenkenson,
> hanged as a witch, 1612

It is not as if God has abandoned you
two feet above the ground, your dress shoes
laced sharp as lancets. Here *Passiflora Incarnata*,
passion vine, the corona thorn-like, a yellow fruit
narcotic belief. Of flower sorts. There a man
metering death in word.

Did you push the peony seeds
into your pocket? Write your confession
on parchment with red ink, roll it
among petals? Did you hide it
in the linen chest? Burn it in the garden?

All is ritual: Evenings you untied your hair, pulled
your fingers through night's likeness, mornings
kneading the dough to flesh suppleness, and now
the ground around you is sprinkled in holy
water—rosemary, thyme, verbena, salt. *Dei judicium,*
anima Christi, anima humana. This is a trial by ordeal,
and thirst is merciless, earth another body
gravely in need of you.

Woman Trapping

The day after the funeral, dress changed to pants,
I kneel hard before the woods
with the rifle my uncle handmade and left me,
rubbing it down with mutton tallow, disguising the scent,
preparing to make the trek through his trap-line
with Aunt Hattie's directions, *look for them notches*
h'at the base a trees.

The trail begins between walnut and elm,
my fingertips and palms shiny over the rifle's stock,
his trap bag pressed against my breast, the advice he gave me
two days before he died, working through my head—
Li'l Indian, a hunter needs to be a bit bigger
than the string he uses to tie up his pants.
He. His.

On the trap-line, so out of practice,
I cannot tell if the catbird calling is male or female,
and regret I am not a nest-builder
or some other creature more clearly determined.
Under the catbird calls, I see a young dogwood,
stand next to it, each of us, skin smooth, lines straight.
Decide my sex is *sapling.*

By the end, most traps already sprung, I lie down in the May apple,
T-shirt rusty, and close my eyes, retrace my path.
In my uncle's woods, I conjure my body
first as man and then as woman—how Natives, he taught me,
can redraw their country in dreams.

Carving the Sentence

for V. Crawford

My mind chases rabbits
(I tell my doctor),
draw analogy to her science, to

> the chambers of the heart—
> any valve open I'll

run through, forget
the prolapse, find
the left ventricle,

> end up caught in the ocular nerves.
> *Don't ask me how I got here.*

At home my dog cuts
through the woods,
six acres of possibility,
and a rabbit jack-knifing

corners,

> *sink holes,*

> *cypress knees.*

I hear the breaking brush, the whoosh of leaves, his speed
measured out in the distance
between

> the snap of cane

> and

> the scream, wild,

that stops even me. For a moment
the birds pause drafting lyrics,

> *night lays down*

> *her weaving in silence,*

and none of us know what?

> until the end,

8

                   until the kill
                                  is carried home,
        possum mama,
                            four hairless kits

                                      latched to her teats,
                (no rabbit in sight)
                                  a family to bury.

The pear tree maybe producing this year,
maybe next.

From Pyrrha's Diary, After the Flood

The world is gone, save this small piece
I am standing on, my husband across the way
already gathering stones for the future,
his elegant frame folding like peppergrass.
I would help him, but I am too busy
turning my back on the water,
fascinated that I am still always facing it,
measuring my luck by my reflection in the flood.

He tells me *luck is a small poppy worn in the hair*,
its brilliance a thing of the moment.
He tells me to gather more stones.
He tells me to think of the coming children.

But I am too raw to nurse another child.
Today I wish myself like the other women,
the ones who did not make it, the women
who thought the water was to put out the fire of the sun
for a time, to extinguish the light so their children might sleep,
so their families might take respite from the fields.
How lovely not to have known the pitch of the storm,
the quickening of the water as it circled their torsos.

For Josh Who Thought He Would Not Turn Seven

And the tailor resolved to go forth in the world
because he thought his workshop was too small for his valor.
The Brave Little Tailor, Brothers Grimm

I remember Josh, his first day of summer
school, his damaged hand, hot with infection,
bound in Scotch tape. I promised to remember, had to,
his body so small others might forget where he is, asleep
in the tale of *The Brave Little Tailor*. The pages shine
next to his skin, grease-stained, fingers dark
as the gangrenous flesh of his wound,
            the pull and knot of the stitches
                                    mere ornament.

                        In class, Josh tells me
the Commanche Codetalkers used the word *techa-keena*,
sewing machine, for machine gun.
This education disturbs him, stitches his brow
until the skin of his forehead is a small fist:
            They probably only knew about the needle hole part,
            not the thread part, he says.

And preferring his interest in sewing, in this story
of the brave tailor, in the possibility that all things torn
from the body or within the ragged cage of the chest could be mended,
that even *he* could tailor *this hand*, *this heart* perfectly, he asks

Miss L? Shouldn't machine guns come with thread?

And I say, yes.
            Let everything come with thread.
Childbirth. Thread included.
1984 Chevy Pick-up. Thread included.
Bicycle. Stray cat. Hollypark trailer. Ritalin. Thread included.
Memo to your father: Do not send your child into engines
            to divine the misworkings of your own hands.
            Thread included.

Every birthday, Josh. Thread included.

You will know your stitches by degree of strength:
Line   cross   chain   and satin,
the stitch with the raised finish like a smooth scar, like your lips
when you read, straight as a line on your very own horizon.

Sacra Via

Evenings my mother turned us out
to the porch, a ritual, three children
waiting on the steps, the one hour
for Father to drink his beer, relieve
his bladder, our home remedy against
the cancer that held everything back,
turning his body the yellow-green of a bruise,
a piece of fruit dropped from our clutch.

Children, our hands small, we took turns
doing what we could. I made the meals,
cooked the beans, all I knew at eight.
Beans and water, boil. Butter, salt, pepper
to taste. My mother cooled a spoonful
with her breath, spilled the heavy broth
into her mouth, told me *The beans
need doctored,* and I added more butter.
I could doctor one thing, not another.

My father's body broke down
in spite of me, his muscles turned soft,
his skin thin as the flesh of those beans—
I walked my father's spine, curled
my bare toes into the thinness of his back,
digging in my heel when he asked.
I learned to move the whole weight of my body
into each small step. And what more?
I read from the Bible every night, promised
that we all *believed,* that Father *would not perish,*
that even after this there would be life.

never mind where you are going,
field, fence line, fruit grove, you tell me

every last breath goes this way.

Procession

I recall the yellow house on the bank,
the heavy porch overlooking the park
where sugar maples grew, a maze of trunks
I ran through, breathlessly gathering leaves
and imagining a huge burning pyre,
but could not gather the courage
to sacrifice anything, not even the damaged worm
under the walnut's slow rot.

When father came home from the hospital,
voices were small because nothing could be larger
than his pain, the yellow and green
that filled his eyes and stained his skin
the color of an envious man. So much damage,
the doctors said, before we caught it,
the cancer a wild sweating horse tearing
across fresh crops, farmhands stumbling,
fumbling with ropes.

I think of the white smoke
of his pipe, billowing on the porch,
following the wave of drying sheets;
the smell, heady like honeysuckle,
followed me to school and home again
to him on the porch, the sun radiating
the cloud, brilliant and white,
that rose from his mouth.

Letter to the Postmaster

I do not live in Watertown, Sir,
where a mother is married
to a grey suit hanging in her closet,
where a little girl hides
behind a horsehair couch,
where a hardbound *King James*, yellow
rose pressed in Genesis, lies
open on the nightstand.
I do not live there.

Look for me in my grandmother's fruit cellar,
past the canned peaches, plums
dried on braided cotton string, pears
deep in syrup. The red clay wall will guide you
past apple crates, rough slats, sticky with juice,
air cold, sweet as honey, to a worn cherry
rocking chair, where I wait your arrival.

Suspension

for Alison Stine who asked *how will our hair hold us?*
　　　　　—from "The Wig"

August, in Peru. My hair is falling out.
I scrape it from the pillows each morning,
hold it up, nest cupped in hands, to my husband.
He throws it away, cleans out the shower drain too,
but won't speak of the invisible weight in the house—
the ghost girl I have named in Cherokee *Awaduli, I want,*
who pulls out my hair.

A doctor in La Clinica Anglo-Americana tells me
I have bad nerves. Man to man in a whisper asks my husband
if I'm *willing* in bed. He says, *I don't know. She cries.*
On the white hospital bed, I am part of a galaxy,
the smooth patches on my scalp an open star cluster, Pleiades,
the Seven Sisters fixed shining, nothing for them to hold onto.

Patches turned to brittle rose petals,
a witch from Iquitos tells me *Tu cuerpo contiene*
la mala sombra del espiritu—
I have a sick spirit.
Her cure, elixir of a thousand flowers
and the water from seven churches.
In her reed and dirt room, light squaring off
the afternoon, she pours it on my scalp, chanting
que tu mala sombra del espiritu tenga ojos y no vea,
manos y no te agarre, pies y no te siga,
a prayer I mouth all the way home.

But when the hair continues to fall, I think of the cloth district,
its block-long rows of bald mannequins, streets lined
with hairless women, broken hands, their missing limbs.
And then I think of the circus, the three Russian women who come to Peru
to suspend themselves by their long hair above the lions' pace and wait.
In red bodysuits, the women are fiery iron rods, twisting themselves
into hanging sculpture. Together, they become a braid.

Litany for the Confused

On one side of town there is a woman who wants to be a man,
and on the other side of town her father and a voice that sings
you are a long, long train, you go away, you go away.

At home the woman stands in front of the mirror
where the reflection is always herself, female,
a gendered equation of woman multiplied by woman:
behind her in the mirror another woman waiting,
and behind her another, a familiarity repeated
like beads on a rosary she would never use.

She sinks her body into the leather of a black chair,
divines courage to tell her father by making believe
she is the one letting the sun fall, thinking of it
as a copper penny slipped from her hand
and her turning her back on it, a worthless saffron.

But the day has gone bad with the beans
burnt half into night, with the train lurching out
of the station, with its terrible sound, the words
long and *away* trapped in her chest. She leaves
her father with his pipe in his hands, his body
bent in the mark of a question.

Working the Name Tag Booth at My Fifteen-Year High School Reunion

> *I didn't notice*
> *while I wrote here*
> *that nothing remains of the world*

> Charles Simic, "Invention of Nothing"

Maybe you were the one
who wrote boys' names
inside your closet in orange marker,
scribbled out and changed love
as necessary, hid the evidence
with your brother's poster of Linda Rondstadt.
Or maybe you were the one
who put the chalk in Mrs. Grove's eraser,
looked as confused as the rest of us
as she scarred the dark slate in kite-tails.
I don't know. *Maybe* you were the one.
Maybe you have stolen from Might-T Mart,
slipped past police after witnessing an accident,
made love to your husband's sister and cried afterward.
Maybe. It's possible that you have never made love at all.
Perhaps you have grown ashamed of who you are,
never told people you can't hold a job,
or that you never really learned to read, or that someone
touched you deeply *here* or someone touched you
down there. It's possible.
It's possible that you have made millions
on the stock market, lived winters in Brazil,
or depended on fortune-tellers to help you find happiness.
Or maybe you have been held captive at your own request,
saved a goat from slaughter on a neighbor's farm,
hopped a freight train bound West and ended up in the East.
Maybe. Maybe it's all possible, except this:
You haven't been a writer.
You haven't held a word on the end of your tongue
and tasted its sweetness like honeysuckle,

or its bitter clamp of alum. You haven't been so taken
in the instant between the time the mosquito lights
and the time it breaks the skin
that you have lost your place in a book,
or lost the people who were standing by you
or what little remained of the world.
No, you haven't been a writer.
Your face is too relaxed, your conscience too clean.

Ophelia's Rant Before She Is Heavy with Drink

I *speak like a green girl*,
wear my dress as a turned asphodel,
the petals white, fallen in shards at my ankles.
Don't follow me; my own feet already bleed,
having trailed Hamlet *loosed out of hell*,
offered him quince, access
to the blossoms you had me deny.
You said *declension, into the madness wherein
now he raves*, as if those murky caves
he walks in his mind were both star and abyss,
any place out of my reach.
Father, my arms are as long as the willow,
bent and pouting over the spring creek, the small chubs
spawning and reckless. I may not know how to wreck
less, how to undo stockings down-gyved, distressed
as I have been to keep any terrible bird from the honey
of Hamlet's vows. Näive as you say I am, I will weave
garlands, dead-nettle and crow-flowers. I can do this numb,
unconscious of my hands, the snap of limbs,
the babble of tempting water.

Utility

for Paloma

What draws me to the painting is the woman without hands
kneeling in church, a blue dress wrapped about her,
her stunted arms drawn out in prayer,
or in a task that couldn't be done—
    so many blackberries to be picked.

The title reads *Repose*, but I imagine she must be asking
for forgiveness, having dreamt of her hands somewhere else:
perhaps not among the stems heavy with fruit
but on the body of another woman, that blue dress shed,
wrinkled on the floor like the wasted skin of berries, her hands
maybe slick in the woman's hair, the braids undone.

I have her pray *A woman visited me after the butterfly left,*
and I imagine the wives' tale true, the lover arriving in butterfly yellow,
the sky a dark platter pressed over them, the kitchen fire out,
sugar spilled on the floor and scattered. Jars turned over,
left unwashed in the sink.

But in *Repose* she is confined to that church,
the blue painted folds of her dress, and
that position under the window, the stained glass
that filters in all her red lament, that tells her there are days
when the body is as useless as the mind,
when even a minister's wife is restless,
the fruit cellar filled with berries,
the cow gone dry.

The Nude Photograph

I undress behind the backdrop,
expose the fine bones and flesh,
this filigree of body, newly ashamed
of the shadows on my skin,
newly frightened of the small figure
to be fixed on paper.

You are beautiful, she says. *Beautiful like a thin blade of grass.*

But when she hooks and drops the backcloth,
switches on the model strobes,
turns my shoulders to the glare,
I know I become something else
slouching toward her light—head bowed,
shoulders drawn in, hands overlapped in front.

She adjusts my hips between her palms,
pulls my hands away from me, guides them
straight above, chin up, until I feel perilously suspended
in that light, until I come into focus
in the darkroom, a beckoned ghost returned.

To a Pulaski County Prisoner

Walk to the window in your cell. Look
far past the twisted steel fence, dusty

fields thick with patches of grass, small towns
And their pumpkin festivals.

squint your eyes over Greensborough,
where every night a man lays his hands

on his daughter, where a daughter cannot be
clean enough.   Look at me

in Bates in a salvage yard where your car sits,
folded envelope in the front seat, pictures

of your children, Elissa, Jimmy, your wife, Carla.
Watch me find your list of Inmate Rules, see me

slip your life in my pocket.

Ante Mortem

for C. and K. Armstrong

It is hunting season, and men run their dogs
through the brush, flush out deer to the line of gunfire.

Which man knows what he has lost tonight?

His dog is hit on the highway, legs buckled like broken eaves,
and I am running back for it, unaware of my stumble or my arms
pushing against the night, the low wall of lights
moving toward us—
                                    the two of us, face into traffic.

There is no sound this close to death,
or there is all sound and no sight.
Understand, we cannot bear all of our senses.
                                    Not this dog. Not me.

                    *   *   *

I came crawling down a road once, too, tossed from a car,
the chain finally loosed from my neck, my tongue blue as crow.
All voices, all scrapes, all sound without resonance.
Noise locked in amber
                        or blood, dried in the ears.

Ask the men from the car for other information. Maybe they could see
what I did not, hear what force will discolor skin,
                                    or stop a breath.

Where is there a night not full of the dying?

                            I mean the *before* dead.
The not dead yet. The ones who are just *this* moment
registering the burn of filling lungs, their breath deep with the spring pond,
the ones lying in bed waiting for the daughter to come home,
the ones on the road *bleeding out* after impact. *Out*, the paramedics say,

33

                                        pushing
                                    every nerve to come alive,
come alive, the cornstalks
rough on your face, the sweet smell so thick you must have grown dizzy, good
for you to test us one more time,
                        to outsmart us
                                    behind the house

                                            into the field,
            the four of us running like idiots,
                            arms outstretched,
                                        our shadowed
                                    couples
                        trailing behind.

Unspoken

for C.S. Bailey

I keep tea sets
(See the breadth of this glass cupboard
is more than an arm span across.
If I stand in front, it would take
four of me, from shoulder bone
to shoulder bone, and maybe quiet Aunt Judy too.
I've noticed how her shoulders are smaller than mine,
how she stays hunched up over her angels,
the skeins of white yarn,
blessing each creation for the unexpected guest,
as if through this, she connects herself in light to all people.
I would like to tell my grandson what this means,
that he and Aunt Judy do not understand
family is a distance that travels through bone,
even if the body is in disrepair.
So when he places me near the barn and the pond,
pulls out his camera, and locks me in the frame,
he is only making me into paper, another thread of unreliable light.
I cry not because I'm dying, but because I am moved
by his exhaustive innocence, by his belief in these pictures,
a selective memory that allows him to mark time
and distance.   If he wants a picture, tell him,
he should stand with me in front of my cupboard,
press his shoulder bone against mine,
see how we plot the span of this moment,
my lesson to him, our own history.
You can take the picture.
Make sure it includes that heavy autumn rose tea set)
to have something to fill up
when so much spills away.

Serpent Handling

Agis'e'gwa ani'tsi'skwa
gu'day'wu
adan'ta tsiyatal'sta
ha'ma'ma'

Great mother of the Bird People Clan,
I have sewn myself together.
I lend you my spirit to accompany you.
Let me carry you on my back.

Here in this room I am afraid
        to hear your cracked breath, the hissing
like any machine failing, afraid to say,
        Your long hair, white and tangled across the pillow,
is summer cotton ready for harvest. I stray
        between metaphors, trying anything you may understand:
Agis'e'gwa, great mother, I hold your hands away
        from you. Your fingers are dry and curl between mine,
copperheads through brush. Now you walk *i'nadu-na'i*
        as if serpent handling, as if like a pale woman
who takes up snakes in her arms, comes this close to death and waves
        hands in air, all song in tongue. And this, another room of believers.

Women in Rooms

Room I

The woman nude, white as asters
in front of the bay window,
plays her violin for her lover, the music uncurling
between chin and bowed arm, the furniture
turned away to open a stage free from embarrassment,
but all that glass as her own eye spies on her from behind.

In the music there is a quiver that says she wonders about her flesh,
maybe thinks herself an instrument wrapped thick in tissue,
wondering how she will learn to get her fingers to the strings
of her own body, how she will learn to hear her own sound,
know what to do when the music stops, when she must put the violin down
and walk toward the man on the bed.

Room II

Like you, I know this woman through what is told me,
what is given in word, hushed as sacrament,
how she lies in her bed, her body growing brittle,
each turn a lesson in architecture, how her daughter has learned
to see the beauty in what is left:

The daughter and friends side the bed, gather her body
from the sheets, lift gently, know the chant *light as a feather.*
Grief always awakens memory. The daughter remembers her mother
move through yoga postures, from *Garba Pindasana*
to *Kukkutasana*, embryo-in-the-womb to rooster, *hold*
for five breaths. Now the daughter holds for five;
her mother's ribs have cracked even in this slow lift.
The daughter learns for each posture there is a counterposture—
when one body falls, another must rise.

Room III

For Irtyersenu, who believed in the afterlife, know that
like a mirror in a mirror there are women like this
and rooms of this expiring and somber detail,
that her glass room in the British Museum may replace her home
in Thebes, and that Augustus Granville who dismantled
her mummified body understood the temple of human. Let's say that.

Let's say that—so standing here in front of her,
her body unwrapped and dissected, to her side
her list of ailments before she turned fifty,
the ovarian cyst, malaria, scalp disease, and pneumonia
that killed her, the *carbon in her lungs from domestic fires,*
will read as hangnail, stubbed toe. Let's say that Augustus
does not need to tell us he did everything he could to save her,
that her *lungs, kidneys, spleen, uterus, and heart* are intact—
that he too tried not to disturb the room.

Letter from Peru

for Donna Masini

I dream I can outrun the tornado,
a spinning violence that follows me
across this torn country.
I leap the garbage heaps, the slums,
soar over the women's prison
where they're raising the walls,
the tornado tracing my path.

Peru wins against Chile in soccer,
and the streets erupt into elation,
then fury, a love that is brutal.
One man is lifted above the crowd
and thrown onto the hood of a bus.
His nose breaks open,
and he becomes the screaming red of Peru,
wiping his face on his sleeve,
still waving the flag, *Chilenos, conchas sus madres.*
A herd of people block the traffic,
rock the cars, break the glass.
I imagine the seventy-four hostages
cheer in the ambassador's house.
The MRTA cheer, the police cheer,
a gun takes down a man in the street,
the gun cheers, smokes. This is a love that is brutal.

I dream I can outrun the tornado,
but it turns into a broken woman with blood in her teeth.
She says, *Help me.*
                    Unhook me. Take the parts
and   piece   them   together.   I
                              no longer understand
                                        the logic of sentences.

Everything whirls out of place. The man in the market
copies words onto grains of rice, dropping each

into a glass tube of oil. He sells them as necklaces.

Donna, ask for something small. *I, you, we*. Watching the rice grain
float down through the oil, it occurs to me
not much can be written or stay for that long.

The Writer Who Lost the Word Weasel

for Olga

I tell her there is grief in all loss
and sorry about that and the sleep
she'll miss, too, caught in the bramble
of an alphabet undone, sounds without tails,
kicking each imperfect option back to Nod.

I suggest ferret, groundhog, possum, meerkat,
but she clips, *No, it's we- we-. Small,* she says, *thief,*
drawing on the time between the two words
certainty brings her in his silver box.

What we know and do not know is the same
if we forego the illusion of possession. So we say,
"Maybe it will come back to you," as if words, ideas,
all arrangements of ten thousand things had choice
and we are lovers jilted at an altar in the forest.
Behind us the scurry of syllables shuffle
from cell to veiled cell we are always seeking.

Third Person

for J.

The table cleared, the book put away with the wine,
the story could not be told for the evening.
The storyteller is so beside himself with worry
(his wife always in another room) that he splits desire
and language, speaks himself into the third person,
what one must do, he whispers to me.

I try to believe it does not include me, his speaking of the *one*,
what the *one must do*, convince myself I am not in this story,
but watch it unfold outside as a pear blossom—

> the two lovers pass furtively by the river (the town so small),
> stow away for the afternoon in a distant cabin,
> bend finally together as their own finished sculpture.

But this scene I cannot disown. I, too, am the *one*, the third person
who will pass through his pen onto paper, there intangible
as the trace left of any word, think *cerise*, erased from a line in his work.

I am the splinter removed months ago, a wound
he will always be able to pinpoint, his palm, say,
It was right here; my eyes watered as I finally dug it out,
secretly sorry for its passing or for the trouble his cry had caused,
his apology for calamity, I understand now, *what one must do*.

Nights I stay up late reading, mouth the words
he names me, *inchoate, circling*, see myself
as a blade of grass in the hands of a little boy,
his intense palm-rubbing spinning me back and forth,
a fantastical attempt to start fire from faith

I am the one he attempts to articulate, the woman behind him;
I the third person, the body to be narrated,
a woman unruly as early speech, grammar on the wing.

Tattooed

for V.S.

You call yourself the tattoo lady,
legs patterned in faded paisley
all the way up past your sex.
I have known you to say *Eve* and
laugh into your red wine, holding
the stem of the glass with both hands,
your hair falling like a black sheet
over a line, the line giving to the weight.

But I know you best through your grip
of that dark-handled kitchen knife,
your index finger cocked, knuckles
white and blue, both arms bent rigid
as if you were caught unwillingly
in stasis, as if those arms could not
reach some water's edge, your legs
could not find solid ground, as if paramedics,
frantic in their find, finally drew you stiff
from the lake, your expression anxious, indelible.

III

How can reason reflect water? How
can the swimming child come up for air, her mouth intact?

Swimming the Witch

Used specifically in reference to the ordeal
of witches, 1887—OED

*...pu'd her doun the clachan to the
water o'Dule, to see if she were a witch or no,
soum or drown.* –Merry Men

My friend swings out over the Muskingum on a rope,
herself an obstinate fray, something to pull at.
I am already in the water, ten years old
and neck deep in judgement,
begging her to take the drop, brave like me
jack-knife, cannon-ball, just let go.

Pale in a white one-piece,
she is a length of fine bone dropped onto a plate.
I do not hear her fall. There is no sound of air
trying to heave her back into place,
no warning from the rope thick in its silence,
no voice from the bank calling her home.
Behind her, the afternoon sits back on its haunches.
After her, the water turns still. She does not resurface.

This is how guilt is divined from water—
my days disappear into a warm bath,
into a ribbon of motion as I lie back.
Each time I see my grown body reduced,
refracted small and white. Each time I know
the terror in my grip—Hands wet on the sides
of the tub, as I lift myself free, not free.

Appendix

for Donna Masini

On Halloween in Brooklyn, 1962, your mother makes you
into a geisha girl, spends the day for evening, sewing

heavy silk into a robe, small, fashioning hooks
and a belt to close it. Hide the (   ) of her girl

within. She has already chosen the makeup, organized
the colors across her vanity.

Oh, but your mother is in a flutter, and you are perched
atop the table, face and neck already caked white,

layer of cream, dusting of powder, this deceptive surrender.
Your mother slips the black liner high across your brow,

rubs the red shadow deep into the soft flesh below, covers
the lid heavy green, dark cast of blue. *Don't move,*

I need to make your mouth, she says.
Paints a small red butterfly over your lips.

You are concerned you won't be able to speak, afraid
to break the butterfly in half, think of its dark interior

falling into your mouth. *Say trick or treat and please
and thank you,* as she lifts you nervously from the table,

kisses and guides you out the door. *Don't forget
the words,* she calls, as you totter down the walk, belt tight

around your breath, remembering *all* the words
and refusing to open your mouth, committed to saving
this butterfly, a life you understand is fragile.

Portrait of the Private

Arizona Girl, 3, Survives 5 Days in Car
With Mother's Body (January 27, 2004)
—The Arizona Republic

After the car flips the mother into dark sleep
and the child, rattled from her seat, wakes,

the world can only be small, buckled in steel
as it is. By second morning hunger uncurls

its hand in the girl's belly, and fear reclines
across the backseat. Between them is the private

child knowledge. Not yet the acquaintance of adolescent
girl blood, but female likeness and promises of Tuesdays'

ice cream after kinder-gymnastics, after she flips
and tumbles and lands on her feet, bodysuit blue

as her mother's swollen lips. Everything rolls to this present
passed, this dialectic in blue, this mother still

born to her daughter's new life.

Flight

for Mariposa Lopez

Because in English your name is *butterfly*,
I think I understand how you move through your life,
cupping the air with your hands,
straining your face to the sun,
the day opening sharp to your senses
like a cold orange split on a plate.
You are drawn to such sweetness, the fragrance
of the day starting well, the scent of potential
that your wings will carry you again,
never mind tomorrow or the rain, the severe wind
on the horizon.

But tonight the evening shatters in storm
like a glass fallen from the table.
You fly between bedroom and kitchen,
frantic for your stolen bag, your wallet gone.
You know, you say. *You know*, and I do.
Goodness doesn't separate us from misfortune:
someone's foot will find the shard in the grass,
that broken champagne bottle against the grill,
jetsam from someone else's good luck.

Outside, a wailing train splits the town,
its long dark body rushing wingless,
scrambling down a path you know it will repeat.

On Hands

November, I take Reiki treatments in a dying woman's
guestroom. Dark, there is a slow burn from a candle in the corner,
a hummed prayer over my head.

> *In a previous life, I was a war nurse. Now I dream my arms amputated*
> *in a ward of handless men.*

Hands I cannot see trace the length of me,
my awareness a belief in the static of the body,
the way a mother in the dark hallway of her house
will turn suddenly to find her son reaching up, cannot sleep.

> *Have you read that story about the man who couldn't control his hands?*
> *If we didn't have hands, you know, we wouldn't need pockets.*

In the healing room, the Reiki master tells me my chakras are uneven.
I am a limb broken across another in a storm.

> *That girl cut her sister's hand off*
> *at the woodshed. I'm sorry.*

The woman listening from the other room,
her body piecing off parts to cancer,
says the broken limb is a death wish,
tells me *If you want to die, we will race for it,*
wager a pound of aduki beans
not to see the end of January.

> *Do dead people always cross their hands?*

She makes rules—*We keep our own diets.*
She takes back the tea bark and roots,
the roasted sesame and cashews ground into paste,
the bread of oats and spelts, the millet and molasses.

She takes my pound of aduki beans and pairs it to hers.
God is nuts, she laughs, and lights a candle from her bed.

> *A blind woman on an Ohio farm*
> *palms barbed strands of fence,*
> *searching for broken wire*
> *and the lost calf (behind her, asleep*
> *in hunger).*

Leaving, I run my hands over my ribcage,
another set of fingers bent like fists
around my lungs, left fist firm over my heart.

Half-Hanged Mary Dreams Only Last Lines of Poetry

for Tom Andrews and Amy Newman

1
and nothing would stop the dreams of men wrestling fish.

2
Lord, tending one hungry child after another.

3
as if it were your own hair you'd fly into.

4
A woman labors in the night.

5
Me? I'd turn that piece of hair into a whole man.

6
the hour. This naming of things.

7
her body cut from a sow's ear.

8
the tired dialogue of my four-chambered heart.

9
placing ginseng under his tongue.

10
and sometime after, the rooster killed the dog.

11
in the name of Magdalene.

12
broken. Smile and spit back.

The Documented

In the ditch outside the women's hospital,
graves of stillborns around him, my husband holes up
with his camera, the villages in front of him
impenetrable thickets, and the memory of our house
underexposed, dark as hunger,
                                        the deep hollow of the belly.

In one house a man and woman lie
on the floor, their child and a loaf of bread
between them. The man listens for artillery,
measures the time
                        between noise   light,
                                        and
how my husband, too, captures peril
                                        in chrome,
frames the descent
                        of everything
                                        from his point of view:
country,
        home,
                family,
                        woman,
                                wife.

        Side note (guidelines for good photographs): *Watch*
        the massing and placing of shapes and forms
        as they interweave and change in the viewfinder;
        do not allow technicalities to come between you
        and the subject. Do not feed or mend. Document
                                        the tragedy

one troubled place after another
                                        and another, the sky brewing
        over him missiles
                        falling
                                from the night
                                        like stars

                                                    toppling,
like myself,
                my
                        unraveling   self,
                                        Cassiopeia
                                                Collapsing
                                        finally from her chair.

The Science of Guilt

For every action there is an equal
and opposite reaction.
—Sir Isaac Newton's Third Law of Motion

Leaning the cardboard back
onto the shaky body of that one-room house
is a lesson in misunderstanding.
Face it. When you stoop over the earth,
your thin body arched across that shovel
like a daughter you've been protecting all your life,
there is a law of energy that guides you, us,
and a man who mouthed it, who first understood
we will pay for all our actions,
even the ones we only dream about.

I cannot count the forces against you,
the wind, the brooding rain, the landowner
who asked you to work for six dollars a day,
but I can tell you I, too, have tried to ignore the weight of things,
my own hair as it slipped from my head as I slept,
the pillow it landed on, the feather-tick bed beneath it,
and that heavy stone wall around it,
the one place where our lives connected,
where you stayed, I left.

Heidegger's Student, Unsettled

for J.

Like the swallow, we construct the world—
an enormous nest...of two sorts of time,
one we can dispose of and one that is lacking.
      —Boris Pasternak

She sits on her knees above the river—
the white and blue pressure of bone
beneath her skin like hesitant morning.
In the stirring river bottom, silt speaks:
I am Magnolia limb, minnow, the sinew of vine,
                              the awfulness of disrepair—

(By what language other than fragmentary—
other than the language of shattering,
of infinite dispersal—can time be marked?)

There was a time the woman remembers
when her lover swam just under that river's
                              surface, shoulders
                                        dividing the current,
watery fingers over his back.
                    Breaking

may happen without sound—this man
                              undoing the stream—all the pieces sign
language, signing

          Let me give a little hint on how to listen:

          Breaking

may happen without sound—this man

                                     undoing the self—all the pieces sign

language, signing to the woman

See? This day will bleed too, embryonic and already angry.

Limb by Limb

I

The night the woman child was born
into a house with a porch that stuck out
like a tongue waiting for medicine,
there was definition—
that the white-with-blue-speckles
wash pan was placed just left
center of the table, that the heavy cotton
curtains, stained rose, were pinned
shut, full with the wind,
that the eldest sister could turn
away from the doctor, away
from her laboring mother and think
The beans need to come off the stove.

But no one thought the word *hard*
in this house where the wooden floor
was not flat, where the kitchen spilled
into the living room, downhill
to the bed against the wall.
The mother thought of *butter,*
of the three gallons of milk
she churned, the bearing down
of broom handled into bucket,
the stiffness of her limbs afterward.

II

In 1935 she wore brown
and carried fallen corn from the field.
Her feet curved around the clumps of soil,
the husks curled around her back.
And she, like the horse who has never tasted
summer grass, looked neither left to the water
nor right to the field, but kept her pace, steady,
for the house, the bees swarming at her wet neck.

She cleaned the dinner fish, slipping the hickory
blade through the belly, the eggs dropping
to the table, the liquid dark drying on her hands.
It was the first summer she found herself
heavy with child, and lost it, falling
from her, a velvet clump, something like night
but viscous.

III

The eldest sister filled a jar
from the well and turned back to the house
where the fire swelled under the bread, steak
softened in gravy. She split an onion,
dropping the quartered sections in water,
placing the bowl on the table, scooting it
just out of reach of the children.

The doctor moved from the table
to the bed, his thick body sore
from the ride, his rough hands leaving
behind the knife. The woman child's head
pushed into the room, into the house,
toward the porch, her curved shoulders
holding up everything before them.

Venerari

Last night when I couldn't sleep, I drank cough syrup,
cough syrup with codeine, enough to put a raging dog on its side,
or even a raging Pope. That's what I thought about
thirty minutes after I drank it, the Pope high on codeine cough syrup,
blessing the liquid, red and oily as blood as it passed down his throat:
Laude cough syrup, turning the spoon from the bottle to his mouth,
Laude codeine, spilling the liquid across his perfect tongue
into his perfectly human body.

Worship is the same no matter where we are.
There is always something to love, and always someone
to love it. The idea never changes.

My brother and I secretly swam in the baptismal on Wednesday nights
while my father prepared his sermon, the cool water closing in
on our small naked bodies like sugarwater overtakes fruit.
It was a sort of worship, our skinny paleness floating back and forth
across the water, we giggling and shushing each other when father's voice
echoed across the pews. Our shriveled hands sent water into the air,
and we praised everything that made those evenings possible.
Praise you, sister! my brother called out, his arms spread apart,
palms up, his face turned skyward, water sliding off him,
the image of any miracle first discovered. I was in awe of him.
Praise you, brother, I responded. *Praise you.*

Pantoum for a Roane County Childbirth, 1942

When the good doctor needs to be fed,
slit the belly of a squirrel, the skin cut from the muscle.
When the laboring woman cries out, do not go to her,
but bring the knife solid, low through the squirrel's neck.

Slit the belly of a squirrel, having cut the skin from muscle
in smooth strokes, keeping the hide taut.
The knife already clean through the squirrel's neck,
slip the blade through the hip and shoulder, left then right,

in smooth strokes, hide taut, throw the tail to the cats.
When the laboring woman cries out again, do not go to her,
but watch the slip of hip and shoulder, left then right.
Rinse the body in drawn water; leave the bucket at the well.

When the laboring woman cries out again, do not go to her,
but roll the body of the squirrel in flour, fix it in cast iron,
the body drawn across the skillet, fat welled into curves,
into the flour and hot grease, milk added, finally gravy for four.

Fix the squirrel on a plate. Stack fresh sheets on the cast iron bed
for the laboring woman who has called out all day,
knuckles white as flour, forehead hot, her milk spilled (her child's gravy),
when the good doctor needs to be fed.

Final Notes

> Hay mucha muerte, muchos acontecimientos funerarios
> en mis desamparadas pasiones y desolados besos,
> hay el agua que cae en mi cabeza,
> ....
> oigo que alguien me sigue llamandome a sollozos
> con una triste voz podrida por el tiempo.
> —Pablo Neruda, "Oda Con un Lamento"

After Joyce leaves a note on my desk,
Make sure you smile today,
I write back, tell her *Things tend to awaken*
even through random communication—
Her cursive is a scattering of broken choke vines,
my letters, tight wasps, curled into themselves,
each word, a day's dying on the window sill.

When she asks *Where does energy come from*
if we can't get it from caffeine? I scribble back, *Poetry*—
Can't you see your own arms as thin stalks,
your hands, red tulips? (How she might lean
out the window, lift to the light.)
There. That saucer of light.

Friday, these directions on my desk:
L, the word 'bikini' comes from a Pacific island
where they tested the hydrogen bomb.
Look up 'hydrogen bomb'; read instead 'bikini.'

I take the bait, look up hydrogen bomb, read:
> *A bikini is a weapon deriving a large portion*
> *of its energy from the fusion of lighter elements*
> *to form heavier elements. The bikini's success*
> *lies not only in the differences in the body's mass*
> *which converts to energy, but the extremely high*
> *temperatures required to initiate bikini reactions.*
> *These explosions are remarkably more volatile*
> *depending on the thickness of the bikini's outer layer.*

Theorists continue to argue the ethical use of the bikini.

Monday. *Dear Joyce, I swim nude,*
                    (avoid bikini politics).

Tuesday. The word *Don't* glares from a post-it on my desk.

Later, I stand in the rain, watch the ground swell with water,
a tree absorb so much that it cannot bear its own body—
listen to the deep groan of the roots as it falls, the heaviest sigh
in the world. To survive we must make ourselves bone dry—
No derrumbarnos desde la piel al alma, avoid our own collapse
from skin to soul.

There is a pause in our note passing (*nothing* to put in italic),
and we never speak, slip like water on opposites sides of pine.

Then this from her: *This morning I considered a mystifying
disappearance, carnivalesque, pulling the blankets over my head.
L, I wanted to be gone, but I could not fool myself.
You know that even the dead return to the earth.*

All weekend I've been thinking of this—
random disappearing acts, slow as they are between us,
as if the shower water or the rain over the trees or either of us
melts us down to bare topiaries.

I write back: *Joyce, a friend called me, told me 'God is stupid,'
told me 'he throws one dying woman on another's dying lap.'*

I haven't heard from Joyce in days, but it's okay. I will *suddenly proclaim spring*
to save her. I will give her one of my ribs, welcome her back.

Post Mortem

The condemned pitches herself headfirst, again, into water,
    a lake so still
        she believes
            it is the iris, blue, of her eye.

        (Plucked and tossed)

She somersaults to a stiff glide, her entrance
            smooth, barely
              a ripple.

In this death she is the plucked eye she is the angel of her sight—

    She sees her cat uncoil in the sun, its leg
           combing a patch of yarrow, beetle
        s c u t t l i n g   from reach.
    She sees words—
      The grasshopper's wing, that yellow, the slur of dust.
                Salt

      (scattered at her front door) Warning: *Devil's woman. Witch*

Which hand to love god curled in rope wrist(ed)
           red is wit

(*witan/witega/wicce*)

          a myth gathering
             around her throat

    to breathe in water
       to walk from fire

Notes

"Letter from Sussex" is based on multiple histories of witch trials and persecutions included in *Witchcraft in Europe: 1100-1700, A Documentary History* and *The Catholic Encyclopedia, Volume XV* on witches.

Epigraphs to sections I, II, and III are from "Nocturnal Reel" and "Bramble Portrait" in *On a Stair* by Ann Lauterbach.

Information on passion vine and peonies in "Station of Loss" comes from *Green Magic*, by Morwyn.

"Serpent Handling" incorporates Cherokee. The untranslated phrase *i'nadu-na'i* means to go in the company of a snake.

"The Other Lesson" responds to Donna Masini's poem "The Lesson" in *That Kind of Danger*.

"Ophelia's Rant Before She Is Heavy with Drink" incorporates text from William Shakespeare's *Hamlet*.

"Utility" includes the folklore of the butterfly whose appearance in one's home indicates the upcoming arrival of a lover, noted in Hans Biederman's *Dictionary of Symbols*.

The italicized text in "Letter from Peru" is from "Looks That Kill" in *That Kind of Danger*, by Donna Masini.

"On Sunday, Marion of Orkney, Accused Witch, Plants Hysteria" is based on the transcribed experience of Marion Cumlaquoy of Orkney who was burned in 1643 for turning herself three times *widdershins* (counter-clockwise) to make her neighbor's barley crop rot.

"Heidegger's Student, Unsettled" incorporates text from Martin Heidegger's *Being and Time* in lines 7-9 and line 19.

"Women in Rooms": Lines 2-3 in Part III are from "The Praxis of Breast Cancer" in *Order, or Disorder* by Amy Newman. Italics in lines 10-11, 14 are from Irtyersenu's exhibit in the Egyptian section of the British Museum.

"Litany for the Confused" incorporates a line from Paolo Conte's original song, "Dragon," from *The Best of Paolo Conte*, Nonesuch Records, 1998.

"Half-Hanged Mary Dreams Only Last Lines of Poems" is based on the accounts of Mary Webster (late 17th C) who was accused and hanged for being a witch. Several witnesses bear testimony that she survived the night and was thus cut down and released the next morning.

"Final Notes": Italics in lines 3-4 and line 49 come from Robert Creeley's poem "The Conspiracy." Italics in line 13 come from C.D. Wright's *Deepstep Come Shining*. Information on the word bikini and the hydrogen bomb has been referenced and adopted in variant form from *The Concise Columbia Encyclopedia*. The Spanish has been adopted from Pablo Neruda's poem "Solo la Muerte" ("Death Alone").

"*Post Mortem*": The line "The grasshoper's wing, that yellow…" is from Charles Wright's poem "Yellow" in *Hard Freight*. The words *witan, witega, wicce* are early derivations of both *witch* and *wit* found in *Skeat's Etymological Dictionary*. The color red is historically equated to witches in Scottish folklore—witches were believed to take the form of red butterflies.

Leilani Hall received her M.A. in creative writing from Ohio University and her Ph.D. from the University of Southern Mississippi Center for Writers. She is currently Assistant Professor of English at California State University Northridge, where she teaches creative writing and theories of poetry. She has taught at Ohio University, Marietta College, Colegio Roosevelt/The American School of Lima, and was visiting writer at the International School of Bebek, Turkey. Recipient of the Jane Kenyon Prize for Poetry, she lives in Woodland Hills, California with her dogs and butterfly koi.

Printed in the United States
102775LV00002B/149/A

9 781932 339901